Consultant Dr Dennis Ogden
Director East-West Trade Studies
Polytechnic of Central London
Managing Editor Belinda Hollyer
Editor Beverley Birch
Design Jerry Watkiss
Picture Research Diana Morris
Production Rosemary Bishop
Illustrations Ron Hayward Associates
                    Raymond Turvey
Maps Matthews & Taylor Associates
(pages 44–45)

Photographic sources Key to positions of illustrations: (T) top, (C) centre, (B) bottom, (L) left, (R) right.
Barnaby's 30(BL), 31(TL), 31(C). Nick Birch cover, 26(BR). Black Theatre, Prague 23(BL). Bo Bojesen 11(B), 13, 20, 21(TL), 21(BL), 22(B), 23(TL), 24(BL), 27(TL), 27(TR), 28, 29, 33(TL), 33(C), 34, 36, 37, 38, 39(TR), 41. Camera Press 18(B), 19(B), 23(BR), 39(TL). J. Allan Cash 30(BR). Czechoslovak Travel Bureau, London 9(T). European Geographic Survey 2–3. Greg Evans 9(C). Sally & Richard Greenhill 31(TR). Imperial War Museum 19(C). Mansell Collection 16(BL). Military Museum, Belgrade 15(BL). New Albania Society 22(C). Chris Niedenthal 10(TR), 11(TL), 11(TR), 21(TR), 21(BR), 24(C), 25, 26(BL), 31(BR), 35(TL), 35(TR), 39(B). Novosti 18(T). Photosource 17(BR). Polish Tourist Information Centre 40. Rex 19(T). Suddeutscher Verlag 14(T), 15(T), 15(BR), 16(C), 17(T), 17(BL). Tate Gallery, London 23(TR) photo Eileen Tweedy. Tourist Office of the German Democratic Republic 6–7, 121. David Williamson 9(B), 10(TL), 12(R). Zefa 24(BR), 27(B), 30–31, 31(BL), 33(TR), 35(B).

Contents page: the Alexanderplatz, East Berlin

Endpaper: Bulgarian women enjoying a break from work in the fields

A MACDONALD BOOK
© Macdonald & Co (Publishers) Ltd
1979, 1987

First published in Great Britain in 1979
by Macdonald Educational Ltd

This revised edition published in 1987
by Macdonald & Co (Publishers) Ltd
London & Sydney
A BPCC plc company

Printed in Great Britain by
Purnell Book Production Ltd
Member of the BPCC Group

Macdonald and Co (Publishers) Ltd
Greater London House,
Hampstead Road,
London NW1 7QX

British Library Cataloguing in Publication Data

Riordan, James
    Eastern Europe.—2nd ed.—(Macdonald countries)
    1. Europe, Eastern — Social life and customs – Juvenile literature
    I. Title
    947   DJK50

ISBN 0 356 11826 6
ISBN 0 356 11823 0 Pbk

Eastern Europe

the lands and their peoples

James Riordan

Macdonald Educational

Contents

Eight diverse nations

Mountains and plains

Eastern Europe consists of eight socialist countries. In order of size they are Poland, Yugoslavia, Romania, Czechoslovakia, Bulgaria, the German Democratic Republic (GDR), Hungary and Albania. Poland is just larger than Britain, and Albania is about the size of Belgium.

Altogether, these countries cover a third of the area of Europe (excluding the Soviet Union), and extend from the Baltic Sea in the north to the Black Sea in the southeast and the Adriatic in the southwest.

Eastern Europe is an area of many contrasts. The northern parts of the GDR and Poland form part of the flat Northern European Plain which stretches from Holland to the Soviet Union. It is mainly farmland. Czechoslovakia is a mixture of fertile plains and high mountain ranges, while Hungary has some low hills in the north, but consists mostly of the Great Hungarian Plain. Neither nation has any direct access to the sea. Romania is a mountainous land, except for the eastern coast and Danube Plain in the south.

The three countries in the south, Yugoslavia, Albania and Bulgaria, lie on the Balkan peninsula. 'Balkan' is the Turkish word for 'mountainous', which is a fitting description for them, though all three have a lovely stretch of coastline on the Adriatic and Black Seas.

Climate

The climate of Eastern Europe varies greatly. In the northern and central areas it is very cold in winter and warm in summer, while the coastal areas of the southern states enjoy a Mediterranean climate, with mild, rainy winters and dry, hot summers. Some areas, especially in the central and eastern regions, have long snowy winters, with a fairly low rainfall throughout the year.

▲ The High Tatra mountains in Czechoslovakia provide some of the most dramatic scenery in Eastern Europe. With the Low Tatras to the south, they form the western end of the Carpathian Mountains.

◄ Dubrovnik is one of the most popular resorts on Yugoslavia's Adriatic coast. The mountains come down to the sea and form deep-water inlets which make excellent ports like Dubrovnik.

▼ The Hungarian Plain or *Puszta* covers much of the eastern part of Hungary. It is a haven for animals and birds.

Language and people

The Slav 'sandwich'

The map of the Eastern European family is like a sandwich with the Slavs at the top and bottom and non-Slavs in the middle. The northern Slavs comprise the Poles, Czechs and Slovaks, with a tiny island of Sorbs in the GDR. The southern Slavs are the Bulgarians and the four main Slav groups of Yugoslavia: Serbs, Croats, Slovenes and Macedonians. All the Slavs speak a variation of the same language. But over the ages they have grown so far apart as to make it hard to understand one another.

Between the Slav groups are the Magyars of Hungary and the Romanians, who speak a language akin to Italian.

Two other major peoples live in Eastern Europe. In the north-west are the eastern Germans of the GDR, now separated from fellow Germans in the west as a result of the new political boundaries after the Second World War. In the south-west are the Albanians who have kept the language of the pre-Slav inhabitants of the Balkans.

The borders of the different states, however, often do not coincide with language groups; there are many minorities left on the 'wrong' side of the frontier: Albanians in Yugoslavia, Magyars in Romania and Yugoslavia, and Turks in Bulgaria and Yugoslavia.

The two main religions are the Orthodox Church (Romania, Bulgaria, Yugoslavia) and the Roman Catholic Church (Poland, Hungary and Czechoslovakia).

◀ In remote rural areas men and women still wear national costume.

▲ The Jewish cemetery in Prague. Many Jews died during the German occupation and others emigrated to America or Britain. The Jewish population of Prague now is very small.

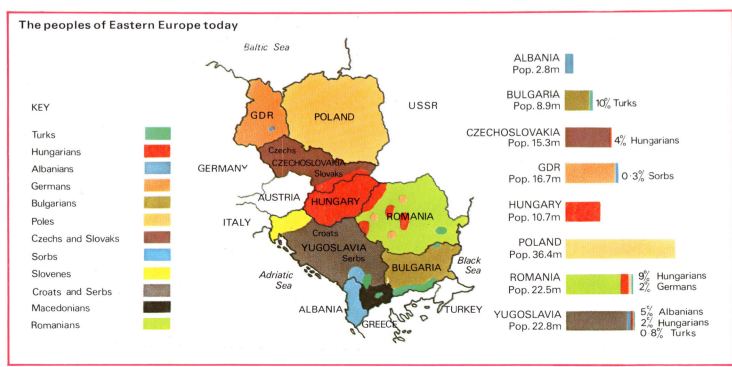

The peoples of Eastern Europe today

KEY

- Turks
- Hungarians
- Albanians
- Germans
- Bulgarians
- Poles
- Czechs and Slovaks
- Sorbs
- Slovenes
- Croats and Serbs
- Macedonians
- Romanians

ALBANIA Pop. 2.8m

BULGARIA Pop. 8.9m — 10% Turks

CZECHOSLOVAKIA Pop. 15.3m — 4% Hungarians

GDR Pop. 16.7m — 0·3% Sorbs

HUNGARY Pop. 10.7m

POLAND Pop. 36.4m

ROMANIA Pop. 22.5m — 9% Hungarians, 2% Germans

YUGOSLAVIA Pop. 22.8m — 5% Albanians, 2% Hungarians, 0·8% Turks

▲ There are many old wooden churches and monasteries in the north of Romania. This church dates from the eighteenth century.

◄ The Roman Catholic Church is very strong in Poland. This is an outdoor mass in a village near Cracow in southern Poland.

▼ This is the interior of a Muslim mosque in Pristina, southern Yugoslavia, where there is a large Albanian population, the majority of whom are Muslims.

11

The crossroads of Europe

Early settlers

Down the ages Eastern Europe has been at the crossroads of trade routes between Western Europe and Asia. It has also been at the centre of the movement of people across Europe.

The ancestors of the present inhabitants of the area settled there mainly between the fifth and tenth centuries AD, after they had been driven out of their homelands.

The Slavs, who form the largest ethnic group today, originally came from central Russia, but were forced westward by attacks from the east. By AD 1000, they had split up into different groups.

The Hungarians originally came from central Asia and settled on the central plain of Eastern Europe from the tenth century onwards.

In the south, the major influence in early times was the Byzantine Empire, which grew from the eastern part of the Roman Empire after it split in two in AD 395. This empire continued until its capital, Constantinople (later called Istanbul), was captured by the Turks in 1455.

The Turks then steadily extended their influence north through the Balkans into Hungary and Romania, creating the Ottoman Empire. The Turks were, however, soon pushed back into the Balkans and German and Hungarian influences again became dominant when the Austro-Hungarian Empire was created.

The Jewish influence has also been strong in Eastern Europe. Jews began moving into the central areas of Poland and Lithuania from the twelfth century after persecution drove them out of Western Europe. They formed a large part of the population of central Europe until the Second World War which resulted in the death of most of the five million Jews of Eastern Europe.

Many of the world's gypsies also live in this area, especially in Czechoslovakia, Hungary and Bulgaria. They made their way up from northern India at the end of the tenth century, initially settling at the eastern edge of the Byzantine Empire. But when the Turks advanced northwards, the gypsies moved up through the Balkans.

The Hungarians now occupy a much smaller area than they did at the height of the Austro-Hungarian Empire. In fact, over three million

▲ The features of many Poles and East Germans are similar to those of Scandinavians, with fair hair and skin. This is a group of GDR children with their teacher.

Hungarians are today citizens of other states. There is also a large minority of Germans living in Romania, the descendants of German settlers who came to the Transylvanian Alps in the thirteenth century.

The population today is very unevenly distributed through Eastern Europe. Some areas have little industry and the land is poor, especially in central and southern Yugoslavia, Romania and Albania. The most densely-populated area runs through southern GDR, Poland and Czechoslovakia.

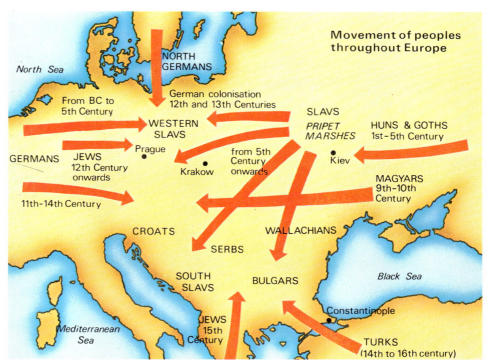

Movement of peoples throughout Europe

▲ Romanian peasants in traditional dress. Romanians are descended from the Roman settlers of 2000 years ago. Their language is like Italian.

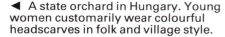

◀ A state orchard in Hungary. Young women customarily wear colourful headscarves in folk and village style.

▲ The central position of Eastern Europe has opened it up to population movements from all directions, as the map shows.

◀ Gypsy girls from Romania. The gypsies call themselves *Rom*, meaning 'The People' and speak Romany in local dialect.

▼ An Albanian from Yugoslavia watches as his horse is being shod. Over a million Albanians live in Yugoslavia, mainly in the province of Kosovo.

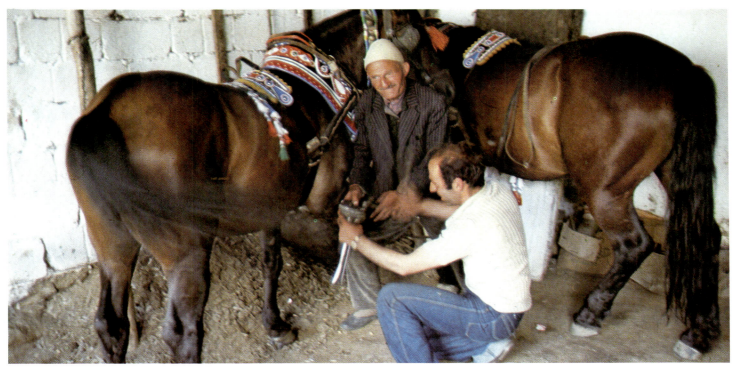

Two empires

The divisions of Eastern Europe

Eastern and central Europe was divided into three main areas in the eighteenth and nineteenth centuries. In the north Prussia expanded eastward along the Baltic Sea, taking over the coastline as far as the Russian border. A unified German state under Prussian leadership was created in 1871.

After the Turkish withdrawal from Hungary in 1699, Austria and Hungary were united under the Hapsburg Empire. For the next two centuries this empire dominated the central part of Eastern Europe.

From the fifteenth century the Turks had been the major power in the south, with control over Adriatic and Black Sea ports as well as over the mineral resources of Wallachia. But in the nineteenth century the Turkish Empire began to crumble. By 1914, Turkey had lost control of all its European territory.

Causes of war

Bitter rivalry existed between the Great Powers of Europe, like Britain and France, Russia and Prussia and Austro-Hungary. It was particularly bitter in the Balkans, especially between Austria and Russia, and this was to lead to the First World War. In June 1914, the heir to the Austrian throne, Franz Ferdinand, was murdered in Sarajevo.

Although the Serbian government was not directly involved in the assassination, Austria accused Serbia of stirring up political unrest in its territories and two weeks later declared war on Serbia. Russia, France, Britain, Belgium, Montenegro, and later Romania, were drawn in, in alliance with Serbia. Bulgaria and Turkey joined Austria and Germany.

While the assassination provided the spark for war, in fact several big powers had long sought an excuse to redivide the spoils of empire and Europe.

▲ After Napoleon's defeat in June 1815, the Great Powers of Europe met in Vienna to establish the frontiers of central Europe. The Congress of Vienna confirmed the position of Austria as the dominant force in central and Eastern Europe, and deprived France of her power.

▼ In 1878 the Great Powers met in Berlin under the presidency of Bismarck to decide the frontiers in south-eastern Europe after the defeat of the Turks by the Russians. The Congress of Berlin split Bulgaria in two and guaranteed the independence of Romania, Serbia and Montenegro, and made Bosnia and Herzegovina Austro-Hungarian protectorates.

◄ The Janissaries formed the first Turkish regular army. Originally they were Christian prisoners forced to adopt the Turkish Muslim religion. In peacetime they acted as a police force and the Sultan's bodyguard. In war they were foot soldiers. They were disbanded in 1826 because they were involved in conspiracies against the Sultan.

► Abdul Hamid II (1842–1918) ruled the Ottoman Empire as Sultan from 1876 to 1909. In 1876 he set aside the constitution which had just been proclaimed and ruled as a despot. He was deposed by young Turks in 1909.

▼ A stamp commemorating the assassination of Archduke Ferdinand and his wife. The assassin was a Bosnian student, Gavrilo Princip, (shown below) a member of a secret society called The Black Hand, which opposed Austrian rule.

► On 28 June 1914 the heir to the Austrian throne, Franz Ferdinand, and his wife were shot dead while on a visit to Sarajevo in Bosnia, at that time part of the Austrian Empire. Austria declared war on Serbia and the First World War began, involving all the big powers.

Collapse of the old order

Between the wars

The defeat of the German and Austro-Hungarian empires in 1918, allied to the Russian socialist revolution in 1917, marked the end of the old political order in central Europe.

Poland became an enlarged, independent state; Czechoslovakia came into being as a totally new state, as did Yugoslavia, adopting the new name in 1929.

During the 1920s and 1930s there was a general move towards dictatorships and, by 1938, only Czechoslovakia could be called in any way democratic. The biggest threat to democracy came from the rise of fascism in Italy and Germany. Hitler, Germany's leader after 1933, rejected the frontier changes brought about by the Treaty of Versailles of 1919. In particular, he wanted to regain those parts of western Prussia which had been lost to Poland, and take over the areas of Czechoslovakia which had a high proportion of German speakers (the Sudetenland).

In 1938 Hitler's armies did take over the Sudetenland, with the agreement of the British and French governments. They then took over the rest of Bohemia and Moravia.

The Second World War

In March 1939 Hitler turned his attention to Poland. When Poland rejected his demands, Germany attacked Poland, after signing a non-aggression pact with the Soviet Union. This time Britain honoured her defence treaty with Poland and declared war on Germany.

Most of Eastern Europe was occupied by the German army during the war. But Hungary, Romania, Bulgaria and Slovakia were allies of the Germans and the Italians. In 1941 Hitler broke his pact with the Soviet Union and invaded it. After bitter fighting, German troops were pushed back by the Soviet Union's Red Army.

In May 1945 Germany finally surrendered to the combined armies of the Soviet Union, Britain and the USA. By then Eastern Europe had been totally devastated by the war and had lost millions of its people. Most of Eastern Europe was liberated from Nazi Germany by the Red Army of the Soviet Union, and this was to play a big part in postwar development.

Of the eight nations of Eastern Europe, five developed initially as part of a Soviet bloc, copying the Soviet system: Poland, Hungary, Romania, Bulgaria and East Germany (GDR). Two, Albania and Yugoslavia, had popular revolutions inspired by the anti-fascist role of the communists during the war, and by the ideals of socialism. Czechoslovakia had a semi-parliamentary road to socialism.

▲ Yugoslav partisans fought a bitter war against German troops during their occupation of Yugoslavia in 1941. This group of partisans was captured and shot in April 1943.

◄ The peace treaty with Germany was signed in the Hall of Mirrors at Versailles Palace near Paris on 28 June 1919. This Treaty of Versailles formally ended the First World War.

▲ The Treaty of Versailles of 1919 set new frontiers for Europe and established the independence of Poland, Czechoslovakia, Hungary and Yugoslavia. Austria subsequently declined as a major European power. The Treaty was also notable in establishing the League of Nations.

Eastern Europe after the Versailles Treaty (1919)

Newly Created States
- Poland
- Free town of Danzig
- Czechoslovakia
- Yugoslavia

— National frontiers after 1919

Czechoslovakia 1919–1939

SUDETEN-
LAND
POLAND
BOHEMIA
Prague
GERM-
ANY
MORAVIA
SLOVAKIA
Bratislava
AUSTRIA
HUNGARY
ROMANIA

Areas with a large German population
Border of Czechoslovakia 1919–1938
Border of Czechoslovakia after October 1938
Area occupied by the Germans after March 1939

◄ After 1919 the border areas of Western Czechoslovakia all had big German-speaking populations. The German leader Adolf Hitler later used this as an excuse for threatening and then occupying Czechoslovakia.

▼ In early 1941 the German army attacked Yugoslavia. Here we see German troops being welcomed in Belgrade by a small number of Germans living in the country at that time.

▲ Hitler enters Karlsbad (now Karlovy Vary) in Czechoslovakia in October 1938. His troops took over the Sudetenland areas of the country in the same month. The Sudetenland had a mainly German-speaking population which generally welcomed the expansion of the German Reich.

▲ Josip Broz, later known as Marshall Tito (right), became President of Yugoslavia. He was leader of the partisan fighters after the country's occupation by German troops in 1941.

Birth of socialist Eastern Europe

Political changes

At the end of the Second World War in 1945, the Allies signed the Potsdam agreement to decide the future of Europe. Now that the Soviet Red Army occupied most of Eastern Europe, communists soon gained political power there.

By 1949 ministers of non-communist parties had been forced out of office, and political systems based on the Soviet model were established. In all countries the Communist Party then became the only party with major political influence.

A certain amount of political unrest resulted from the many political and economic changes. Although working people were in a much stronger position under socialism, they objected when too many sacrifices were demanded.

In the GDR in 1953 and Hungary in 1956 a political revolt had to be put down with the aid of Soviet troops. Many people fled to the wealthier West. In 1961 GDR borders with West Germany and West Berlin were sealed to stop the drain of skilled workers. In 1968 an attempt to introduce a more liberal type of communism in Czechoslovakia was ended by a Soviet-led invasion, and in the early 1980s political unrest swept Poland and an opposition movement called Solidarity grew up, led by a Gdansk shipyard worker, Lech Walesa.

Warsaw Pact and CMEA

Despite the setbacks, the communist system is now firmly established in Eastern Europe. All the countries, except Yugoslavia and Albania, are members of a military alliance known as the Warsaw Pact, set up in 1955 to oppose the Western military alliance of NATO.

The same six countries set up, in 1949, the Council for Mutual Economic Assistance for economic planning and integration (often called 'COMECON' in the West). Yugoslavia broke off relations with the Soviet Union in 1948, and although still a communist state, pursues an independent policy. Albania left the Soviet bloc in 1961 and has since gone its own way. In 1972 Cuba became a member and was followed in associate membership by several other countries of Africa, Asia and Latin America. CMEA members trade mainly with each other.

▼ The Soviet leaders Khrushchov and Bulganin visited Yugoslavia in 1955 to try and heal the split between the two countries. These had been bad since Marshall Tito (left) had broken with the Soviet Union.

▲ Soviet influence moved eastwards after 1945. By 1948 all the states of Eastern Europe had communist-dominated governments. The GDR was set up in 1949.

Map legend — Eastern Europe after 1945
- Acquired by the USSR after 1945 from Germany, Czechoslovakia, Poland and Rumania
- Acquired by Poland from Germany after 1945
- Acquired by Yugoslavia from Italy after 1945
- National frontiers after 1945

(Map labels: Baltic Sea, Formerly the free town of Danzig, G.D.R., BELORUSSIA, POLAND, CZECHOSLOVAKIA, MOLDAVIA, USSR, AUSTRIA, HUNGARY, ROMANIA, Black Sea, YUGOSLAVIA, BULGARIA, ITALY, Adriatic Sea, ALBANIA, GREECE, TURKEY, Mediterranean Sea)

◀ CMEA, set up in 1949, forms a large economic community for nations of Eastern Europe and elsewhere. All its trade is done in a single currency – the convertible ruble. Here we see the 'Fraternity' gas pipeline which delivers Soviet natural gas to Eastern as well as to Western Europe.

▼ Troops of five Warsaw Pact countries invaded Czechoslovakia on 21 August 1968 to stop the reform movement led by Alexander Dubcek. There was no armed resistance.

▲ János Kádár, seen here in the centre, became Hungarian leader in 1956 after the Hungarian uprising. He has been an economic reformer in Hungary and is today Eastern Europe's senior statesman.

◀ In February 1945 the three main Allied leaders – Churchill, Roosevelt and Stalin – met at Yalta to decide what should happen after the defeat of Germany in Europe.

Place in the world today

Building communism

All the nations of Eastern Europe are striving to build a communist society inspired by the ideas first set out by the German philosopher Karl Marx (1818–83), one of the authors of the *Communist Manifesto* published in 1848.

After the Second World War the governments therefore embarked on a series of five-year plans to modernize their countries on socialist lines, with public ownership of land and factories. In the countryside the small peasant farms were reorganized mainly into big cooperative farms.

Yet each country developed differently. Some today are relatively wealthy with high living standards, like the GDR; others are relatively poor, like Albania. With the exception of the GDR and Czechoslovakia, after 1945 all the countries of Eastern Europe had an overwhelmingly backward, illiterate peasant population; and all had suffered appalling devastation in the war.

Types of communism

Some countries had a Soviet-type system thrust upon them in the aftermath of the Second World War, as happened in Poland, Hungary, the GDR, Romania and Bulgaria. Others, like Albania and Yugoslavia, had their own popular revolutions inspired by communist ideals.

Yugoslavia's socialism is based on worker self-management and a mixture of private enterprise and nationalized industry. This has resulted in more freedom and independence, but at the cost of some unemployment and inflation. Albania has developed largely on its own resources, with strict political and economic control. Yet it is probably the most egalitarian of all the states of Eastern Europe.

Particularly in recent years, Romania, Poland and Hungary have encouraged private firms and farms. And in foreign affairs, Yugoslavia and Romania both belong to the 'non-aligned' or neutral nations of the world. Like Albania, they are unattached to any power bloc.

The various socialist systems of Eastern Europe have attracted many other modernizing nations in the world, eager to advance rapidly, and to avoid the problems of capitalist development.

▲ The youth organizations often provide volunteers to help with various kinds of work. Here young communists in Yugoslavia are digging ditches in their spare time or vacation.

▲ With so many people moving from the country to the towns, traffic jams, like this one in Budapest, are becoming a frequent sight in the cities.

◀ Wenceslas Square in Prague. Trams are a frequent sight all over Eastern Europe and, like other forms of public transport, are extremely cheap, though often crowded.

▲ University students usually spend a month of their vacation helping on the farm. These Polish students are helping with the harvest during their summer holidays.

▼ With most women and men working, day nurseries look after young children. The nurseries are relatively cheap and are often attached to the factory where parents work.

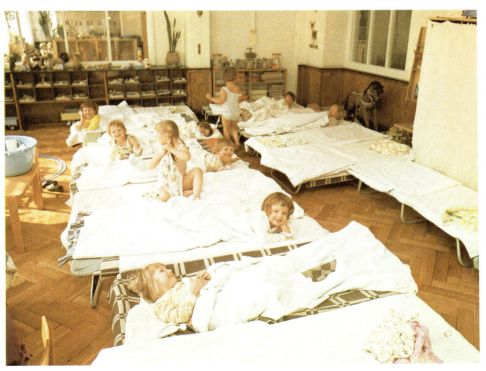

New life in the arts

Artist and audience

In many ways, the arts in Eastern Europe have been brought to the people, made free or inexpensive, understandable and inspiring. Great efforts have been made to educate people to enjoy music and art, drama and poetry. State support has also enabled many talented artists to emerge.

On the other hand, the position of the artist in Eastern Europe can be hard. Writers, film makers and other artists are encouraged to reflect socialist attitudes and aspirations in their work and are not allowed complete freedom of expression. Much of their early work was consequently rather earthy and realistic, but the range has widened considerably in recent years.

The cinema is one form of the arts in which several countries have gained an international reputation, particularly Poland, Hungary and Czechoslovakia. The Polish director Andrzej Wajda is one of the best-known of Eastern Europe's film-makers. He made his first film in 1954. Czechoslovakia's film industry developed later, but soon gained a worldwide reputation with the films of Milos Forman.

The theatre

The theatre has also flourished in Eastern Europe, although it too has had its problems of censorship. As with all branches of the arts, it is heavily subsidized by the state and most theatres are run by local authorities or the state. The aim has been to attract a mass audience by offering a wide variety of light entertainment as well as more serious plays, opera and ballet. As a result, many more people go to the theatre than do so in the rest of the world.

Puppet theatres are a very important feature in the cultural scene, especially in Poland and Czechoslovakia where they are intended for adults as well as children.

Perhaps the most remarkable playwright of Eastern Europe is Bertolt Brecht (1898–1956). He returned to the GDR from America after the Second World War and founded the world-famous Berliner Ensemble in Berlin in 1949. His best-known work is the 'Threepenny Opera', but he is also known for his plays 'Mother Courage' and 'Galileo Galilei'. It is one of the many paradoxes of Brecht's life that he made his chief impact on the Western world, although he created his own theatre in East Berlin, where he lived for the last eight years of his life, and called himself a communist for half his life. He died at the very moment his work was beginning to gain world-wide recognition as probably the central event in twentieth-century drama.

▲ *Ashes and Diamonds* was the last film in a trilogy by Andrzej Wajda about Poland in the Second World War. The film's leading actor was Zbigniew Cybulski (seen here). He died shortly after in an accident.

◀ *News of the Morning*, a painting by the Albanian artist Niko Progri, shows women reading the day's news during a work-break. The Albanian government supports artists with grants.

▼ A Yugoslav artist works on a new cartoon film. These films are very popular all over Eastern Europe, and are sometimes very good works of art. Poland and Yugoslavia are especially famous for their cartoon films.

▲ Constantin Brancusi (1876–1957) was a renowned Romanian sculptor whose works are important examples of abstract sculpture. This is a figure of a bird.

▲ Eastern Europe has many art galleries and museums. This Romanian art gallery in Bucharest has much modern art.

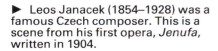

▲ The Black Theatre is famous in Czechoslovakia. Actors perform against a black screen wearing fluorescent clothes; objects on stage are also fluorescent.

▶ Leos Janacek (1854–1928) was a famous Czech composer. This is a scene from his first opera, *Jenufa*, written in 1904.

Preserving old customs

A rich tradition

The customs of Eastern Europe are many, rich and varied, reflecting the wide range of peoples and traditions. The various governments greatly encourage folk art and folklore. Although this is often done for the sake of tourists, there is also a feeling that it is important to keep alive the old traditions despite the social and political changes of the last 40 years.

▲ The formidable Bran Castle in the Transylvanian Alps is supposed to be where the original Dracula lived. Prince Dracula, Vlad III, was famous for impaling prisoners on stakes.

Except in the very remote parts of Eastern Europe it is unusual to see people wearing folk dress in everyday life. But singers and dancers often wear national costume at celebrations such as weddings. These costumes are usually hand-made and require a great deal of skill and patience to make. Folk dancing is also a common sight during festivals, and most of the countries have national folk-dancing troupes which make tours abroad.

Associated with these folk traditions is a whole range of crafts which are still practised today. Handweaving is particularly popular in the southern countries, where wool is in plentiful supply. Woodcarving and basketwork are other popular crafts.

The Village Museum in Bucharest shows the whole range of Romanian folk art in its original setting. In this open-air museum old village houses built in the styles of the various regions of Romania contain many examples of folk tradition.

New customs

May Day, held on 1 May, is a new big celebration throughout Eastern Europe. It is a national holiday when large parades of workers and soldiers march through the major towns. In the past the emphasis was on the military aspects of the parades, with processions of tanks and rockets. Today the emphasis is more on civilian processions, and the whole day is treated more as a festival for the family.

Another important event in the calendar is the Day of Liberation from the German Nazi occupation. This holiday takes place on different days in the various countries according to when that particular country gained its freedom from the Germans in the Second World War.

New Year's Day in most of the countries is more important than Christmas, and most people have New Year's Eve as the occasion for the biggest parties of the year.

Most countries also have festivals to mark the coming of spring, usually at the beginning of March. In the wine-growing lands there are wine festivals, usually in September, to celebrate the harvest.

Many festivals and customs have come down from pagan and Christian times. Today, as elsewhere in Europe, religion is on the decline. But the Church, especially in Poland, continues to derive strength from its close ties with traditional culture and nationalism. In most states the Church has an uneasy relationship with the authorities, but has learned to co-exist.

▲ Popular festivals often have a strong element of folk custom. This is the Festival of Masks in Bulgaria.

◄ This Hungarian woman is wearing the beautifully-embroidered lace blouse that is common with women. She is decorating pottery with a floral design like that on her blouse.

▲ This painting is called *A Winter Scene*; it is by the Polish artist M. Korsak and displays the simple, strong lines of folk art.

▲ Folk dancers in southern Poland. Folk dancing is an important part of popular culture all over Eastern Europe.

◄ The Jews have had a big impact on the folk traditions of Poland. This is an example of Jewish wood carving.

New methods of farming

Farming old and new

Farming conditions vary widely throughout Eastern Europe and differences in climate and geography strongly affect agricultural development. In the north where the land is flat, it is much easier to set up large farms, while in the hilly areas of the south and east large-scale farming is quite difficult.

State-owned farms, farmer cooperatives and private family farms coexist in varying proportions. After the Second World War, many East European governments introduced collective farms based on the Soviet model, whereby the land, machinery and most animals became cooperatively-owned property. The farmer was allowed to keep a number of animals and a small-holding for growing vegetables.

The state farm is most common in Czechoslovakia and Romania where it accounts for a third of all land. These farms are owned and financed by the government, and farmers are paid a fixed wage, as in a factory. On a collective farm the farmer is paid according to his or her work and the total amount the farm earns.

Private farming is still important in most countries, especially Poland and Yugoslavia, where the bulk of production comes from private farms. Even in Romania, where a large amount of the land has been collectivized, nearly 40 per cent of all produce comes from private farming.

Although private farming is tolerated and sometimes encouraged, farmers often have to wait until collective farms have been supplied before they receive their supplies. Much of their produce must be sold direct to the government, but they are free to sell part of their produce privately at open markets.

Produce of Eastern Europe

Eastern Europe produces a wide range of agricultural produce. Particularly important are wheat and barley, sugar beet and potatoes. Maize is also a major crop in the south and central Europe. Poland has the highest output of potatoes in the world, and some splendid wines are exported from the warmer lands like Hungary, Bulgaria and Yugoslavia. Hungary is well known for its *tokaj* wines, and Yugoslavia for its refreshing *riesling* wine.

Productivity in East European farming is generally lower than in Western Europe. For a long time after the Second World War investment in farming was low compared to that in industry, and this meant that farms in most countries lacked modern machinery and fertilizers. As a result, cereal and milk yields tend to be lower for the whole region than the average for Western Europe.

Only recently the bulk of the population in most East European countries worked on the land. The whole area is still far more rural and farm-oriented than most of Western Europe. Of the eight East European nations, only in the GDR are more people employed in industry than agriculture, even today. So the majority of the countries are still developing economies, with many stresses and strains of industrialization.

▲ Albanian women hoeing the land using tools that have not changed for centuries. Albania is now making a determined effort to modernize its farming methods and machinery.

◀ Methods on private farms have not changed as much as those on state and collective farms. This private farm is largely devoted to pig-breeding and is situated south of Warsaw in Poland.

◄ Flocks of sheep in Yugoslavia are often tended by the younger members of the family. These sheep have been marked with the national symbol of Yugoslavia: the star and crescent.
As in the rest of Eastern Europe, about half the working population of Yugoslavia is engaged in farming, but they contribute only a quarter of the national income.

▲ Although most farms in Poland are privately owned, usually by families, there are a number of state farms where the level of mechanization is much higher than in the private sector. State farms are also much larger.

▼ Farm workers in a maize field on a Hungarian collective farm. Most Hungarian farms are either collective or state farms. Only some 15 per cent of the arable land is farmed privately, although the amount has increased in recent years. As elsewhere in Eastern Europe, most farm workers are women.

Industry and technology

An industrial force

Without doubt the countries of Eastern Europe have seen far greater changes in the last 40 years than the more advanced nations of Western Europe whose industries developed in the nineteenth and early twentieth centuries. Modern industrial complexes now exist all over the region and have drawn many workers away from the land.

Efforts are being made to export a wide variety of goods. Poland, for example, is one of the largest shipbuilding nations in the world, while Hungary has the world's largest bus-making plant. The GDR has advanced to twelfth place in the world in industrial growth and is world famous for its precision engineering, particularly at the Zeiss factory in Jena.

Eastern Europe has linked its oil, natural gas and electricity so that each country may benefit. Except for Romania, the region is largely dependent on the Soviet Union for oil and natural gas. The 'Friendship' Pipeline between the Soviet Union and the countries of Eastern Europe supplies their oil needs. Also electric power lines have been linked in an integrated grid system.

The region is a major coal-producer, with Poland one of the largest producers of coal in the world and the GDR the world's biggest producer of brown coal (lignite).

CMEA

In 1949 the Council for Mutual Economic Assistance (the CMEA, sometimes called 'COMECON' in the West) was set up. It comprised all the countries of Eastern Europe except Yugoslavia, plus the Soviet Union and Mongolia. In 1962 Albania left, and ten years later Cuba joined; Vietnam joined in 1978. The aim of CMEA is for all member-states to work to an integrated plan for developing the whole region, in which each member concentrates on what it can best produce, so avoiding wasteful duplication of effort. The trade of CMEA members is mostly among themselves.

Industry and state

Almost all the important industry in Eastern Europe is owned and run by the state. Individual factories have largely worked within a system in which most of the major decisions are taken by central government, except in Yugoslavia.

Recently, however, there has been a move towards greater responsibility for individual factories, especially in Hungary. This has meant that wages now depend much more on how successful the factory is, and this has led to greater productivity and efficiency.

On the whole, the nations of the world with the highest standards of living are those that have completed their industrial revolutions. The nations of Eastern Europe are in the middle of theirs. Communism offers a means to this end, but demands the sacrifice of many comforts and liberties to ensure the job is done as quickly as possible. On the other hand, state ownership of industry has meant that there is no unemployment, virtually no inflation, and fairly rapid industrial and urban development.

▲ Computers are being used in many branches of the economy because of the centrally-run systems and the importance of technology in modernizing economies. Despite American attempts to prevent them, Western firms are helping the countries to develop computers.

▼ An oil refinery at Ploesti in Romania. Ploesti is the centre of the Romanian oil industry, which is the biggest in Europe after that of the Soviet Union. Romania is self-sufficient in oil and natural gas and exports its surplus to many countries in the world.

Eastern Europe's Mineral Wealth
— Oil pipelines
┈┈ Finished products pipelines
◉ Hard coal
🔴 Lignite (brown coal)
🟢 Oil
⚫ Other major industrial areas

▲ Coalminers in southern Poland. Poland acquired the rich coalfields of Silesia from Germany after the Second World War, and is now the world's third largest producer. Poland's mines are equipped with the most modern machines.

▼ Fiat cars being manufactured under licence in Poland. Several Western car firms, such as Fiat and Renault, now have such licensing agreements.

Capital cities

Rebuilding from war ruins

The capitals of Eastern Europe are among the world's most beautiful cities: Budapest and Prague, Sofia and Bucharest, Belgrade and Berlin, Warsaw and Tirana. Yet after the Second World War most lay in ruins. Since then they have arisen from the ashes, like the phoenix, lovingly restored and embellished with new, modern shopping centres and apartment blocks.

Poland and the GDR were the two Eastern European countries most affected by the ravages of war. Before 1939, Warsaw was one of the most beautiful old towns in Europe, built mainly during the seventeenth and eighteenth centuries. After the war most of it lay in ruins. The question was whether the old town could be rebuilt in its former style.

Fortunately there were in existence drawings and paintings of the whole of the old town by such artists as Canaletto. Architects could use these as a basis for reconstruction plans, especially for the facades.

The reconstruction was started almost immediately after 1945, and by 1953 the old town market square had been completed. This was an enormous undertaking, particularly during the most difficult post-war years.

Berlin

At the end of the war, Berlin also lay in ruins. In 1949, two separate German states came into being – the Federal Republic of Germany (West Germany) and the German Democratic Republic (East Germany). The eastern sector of Berlin became the capital of the GDR. Most of the central parts of the city had been badly damaged by bombing but it took longer for East Berlin to clear the rubble and start rebuilding.

With the help of money from America, West Berlin was rapidly transformed into a modern city, but East Berlin received no such aid from the Soviet Union. It was only after the GDR had started successfully to develop its economy in the early 1960s that it could afford a large reconstruction plan. Today the capital of the GDR is the most modern and prosperous of all East European cities, boasting both the splendid renovated buildings of old Germany and the wide modern avenues lined with new shops and restaurants.

▲ Prague is the capital city of Czechoslovakia and lies on the River Moldau. An ancient cultural centre, its university dates from 1348 and it has a fourteenth-century Gothic cathedral.

▼ The city centre of the GDR capital, Berlin. The tall building is the Palace of the Republic which houses theatres, cafes and restaurants. The radio and television tower is 365 metres high.

▲ Bucharest is the capital of Romania. The city lies in the middle of the Wallachian plain and is a major trading centre, especially for oil, timber and agricultural produce.

▼ Belgrade, capital of Yugoslavia since 1929 and of Serbia, lies at the confluence of the Sava and the Danube, making it the gateway to the Balkans, and a big commercial city.

▲ Tirana, capital of Albania, lies 25km east of Durres at the foot of the central mountains. Its university dates only from 1957.

▼ The Old Town of Warsaw was in ruins at the end of the Second World War, but was restored almost exactly as it had been before the war. This is the rebuilt market square.

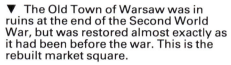

▲ Sofia, capital of Bulgaria, was founded by the Romans, came under Turkish rule from 1382 to 1878, and became the Bulgarian capital in 1879.

▼ Budapest, capital of Hungary, was formed in 1872 by the union of Buda on the right bank of the Danube and Pest on the left.

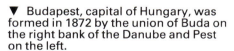

The Danube – artery of Eastern Europe

The Danube as a frontier

The River Danube has been very important in history as a shield against invading armies. For many centuries, it formed the eastern boundary of the Roman Empire. Budapest stands on the site of the Roman fortress of Aquincum, built to repel the barbarian invaders. Today the Danube is a busy and thriving waterway, acting as a link between the countries it passes through. In fact, it is now connected by canal to the Rhine, making river travel possible all the way from the Black to the North Sea, along Europe's two longest riverways.

River at work

The Danube is the second longest river in Europe, 2864 kilometres in length. Only the Volga River in the Soviet Union is longer.

Many of the towns along the Danube's banks are important as ports, particularly for cereals and timber. They include Komarno in Czechoslovakia, Komaron in Hungary, Vukovar in Yugoslavia, Vidin in Bulgaria, and Zimnicea in Romania.

There are also a number of shipbuilding towns, especially the Romanian ports of Orsova, Turnu, Severin and Oltenita which specialize in barges and pleasure cruisers.

In addition there are a number of important industrial towns, particularly the Hungarian town of Dunaujvaros, which has the biggest iron and steel works in the country (the Danube Plant). This huge plant and the adjoining town were only built in 1950 as part of the Hungarian Five-Year Plan.

Other significant economic centres are Bratislava, the capital of Slovakia, Budapest, capital of Hungary, and Belgrade, capital of Yugoslavia. The river empties its waters into the Black Sea in a huge three-armed delta. The Danube is nonetheless not as developed as the Rhine or Elbe, and it carries less traffic.

▲ The Danube traditionally forms a rough dividing line between the southern Slavs (Serbs, Croats and Bulgarians) and the Romanians and Hungarians, who are both non-Slav groups. Today it acts as a national frontier for a large part of its course through Eastern Europe.

In the past many disputes split the countries bordering the River, but they are now working together to improve the Danube as a shipping route. The new canals have helped to increase the volume of cargo traffic.

▲ Barges pass through the lock at the Iron Gate near Turnu Severin. These are the last straits on the Danube before the Black Sea and have always caused navigation problems. Here the Danube becomes much narrower as it flows between the Transylvanian Alps and the Balkan Mountains.

A hydro-electric scheme now controls the flow of water. It is a joint Yugoslav-Romanian project and is one of the largest in Europe.

▲ The beautiful city of Budapest was originally two towns, Buda on the right bank of the river and Pest on the left bank. It became a single town as Budapest in 1872.

► The Danube splits into many rivers and streams before it reaches the Black Sea. The Danube Delta provides a rich habitat for many rare birds and plants. The famous Beluga caviar comes from the sturgeon of the delta.

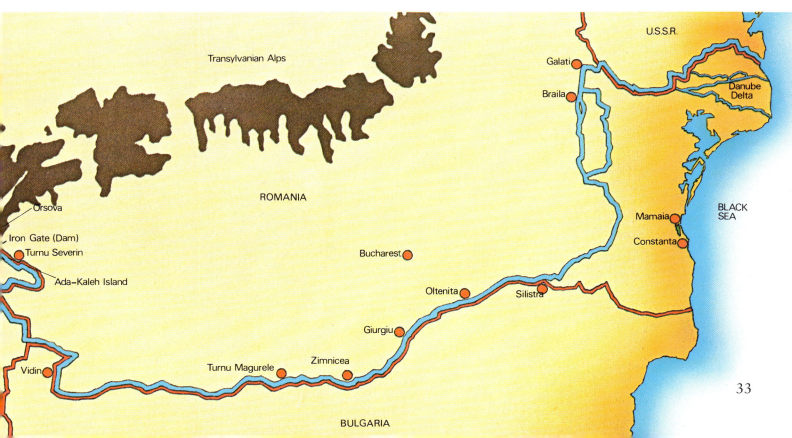

Family life

Drift to the towns

With the industrial revolution, many villagers have moved to the towns, and families have split into smaller units. In the past it was usual for three generations of a family to live together – grandparents, parents and children. It is now more common for young people to move away from home in their late teens or early twenties. It is also usual for both parents to go out to work nowadays, and this means that life can be fairly hectic, particularly as work tends to start early.

Most of the big towns have seen a big increase in population since the war. This, combined with the destruction of many buildings during the 1939–45 war, has meant that all the major cities of Eastern Europe have suffered an acute housing shortage. Some restrict the number of people permitted to enter the cities.

Most people living in towns rent flats. Although many such flats are fairly small by Western standards, their rents are extremely low.

Shopping

Most larger shops are owned and run by the government, with standard prices all over the country. But in several countries there are private shops. These are usually smaller stores offering a particular service like shoe-mending, watch-repairs or hairdressing. All the countries have open-air markets where farmers sell the produce grown in their gardens or orchards. Prices are generally higher than in the state shops, but the quality and range in food and crafts are usually greater.

Prices are more stable than in Western Europe and, with the exception of Yugoslavia, the countries do not suffer seriously from inflation. Certain foodstuffs such as meat and coffee tend to be relatively expensive, while basic foods like bread, potatoes and other vegetables are quite cheap. Clothing and imported consumer durables like cars, shoes and electronics items are usually very expensive and sometimes hard to obtain.

Although living standards are generally lower than those in most advanced Western countries, they are rising and families now enjoy a long weekend and an annual holiday. It may not be long before most families will also have their own car.

▲ A family house in Hungary where half the population still lives in the country and where many houses are privately owned. Sometimes three generations live together.

▼ Although most families in Romania have washing machines, some women still wash clothes in the traditional way – while the men wash the car!

▲ A modern department store in Brasov, Romania. Most large towns have supermarkets and stores in shopping centres.

► Many new housing estates have been built, like this one in Warsaw. All such estates have play areas for children.

▼ An open-air market in Hungary. Each farming family is allowed to keep a smallholding for growing fruit and vegetables. These can then be sold privately.

Food and drink from many cultures

Varied recipes

Wide differences in what and how people eat and drink clearly result from the variation in climate and ethnic traditions.

In the south the Turkish occupation has left its mark on the cooking of Bulgaria, Albania, Yugoslavia and Romania. Here, the food tends to be highly spiced. Pork and beef are eaten, but lamb is the favourite meat with most people. It is often made into different kinds of kebab, such as *shashlik* – pieces of lamb grilled on skewers with onion and green peppers.

In the north the food tends to be heavier, with a high consumption of potatoes and dumplings, and with pork and beef as favourite meats. The influences on cooking in the northern countries have been mainly German and Austrian. Pork dishes are particularly popular in the GDR.

Czechosolovakia's cooking has been strongly influenced by Austria, as can be seen by the popularity of such dishes as *Wiener Schnitzel* (Viennese pork chop). But Czechoslovakia does have some very distinctive national dishes, such as fruit dumplings and carp cooked in garlic, which is the traditional New Year's Eve dinner.

Hungary has one of the most exotic cuisines in Europe. Paprika or red pepper is used in a large number of dishes, such as the world-famous meat stew, goulash, and the excellent Danube or Lake Balaton fish soups.

Polish cooking has been strongly affected by that of Russia, especially in its soups, such as *chlodnik*, a cold beetroot soup.

Wine, beer and 'firewater'

The southern part of Eastern Europe is one of the most important areas in Europe for wine. Hungary is the best-known producer of quality wines, with a tradition of wine-making that stretches back many centuries. The most famous wine is Tokaj, a heavy

dessert wine. Wine is, in fact, a major part of Hungary's exports, though a large amount is drunk at home.

Yugoslavia, Romania and Bulgaria all produce and export large quantities of wine. Yugoslavia is famous for its white Riesling wines, such as the Lutomer Riesling from the north.

All four of the wine-producing countries also make a very strong and fiery plum brandy. The most famous is the Yugoslav Slivovitz. By contrast, the northern countries produce and consume more beer than wine.

Czechoslovakia is the sixth largest producer of beer in the world, and the town of Plzen has given its name to the world's most famous beer – Pilsner. The Germans are also famous beer brewers, and the GDR produces and consumes only slightly less beer than do the Czechoslovaks.

Poland makes and exports a strong vodka – which literally means 'little water'. It is made from potatoes or corn. Vodka is drunk by itself, with nothing added, straight down. Bottoms up! Usually the drinker will at once take a bite to eat: a piece of black bread or some pickled herring, cucumber and onion. Glasses are refilled again and again, until the bottle is empty.

▲ A Romanian woman cooking pastries in boiling oil. Sprinkled with sugar, they taste very much like doughnuts. Such street food stalls are a feature of many towns, adding their appetizing smells to the air.

▼ Poland, as well as the Soviet Union, is famous for its vodkas. Polish vodka is normally colourless, but vodka can be many different colours depending on the basic ingredient.

Some Eastern European foods

▲ Highly-spiced sausage is very popular in all the countries of Eastern Europe. Hungarian salami (left) is one of the most tasty and famous.

▲ *Shashlik* is a very popular form of kebab that is common in the Balkans. Meat, peppers, tomatoes and onions are grilled on a skewer over a charcoal fire.

▲ *Goulash* is a meat stew spiced with paprika which has become popular all over the world. Originally, it came from Hungary.

▲ A wine-cellar in Tokaj, Hungary. The cellarman is testing the wine from barrels that store the wine for several years.

◄ A pub in Hungary. Although the country is a major wine-producer, many Hungarians also enjoy relaxing with a glass or two of draught beer.

► Wine labels from Hungary, Yugoslavia, Bulgaria and Romania are often written in English for export.

Schools and education

Equal opportunity for all

Each country of Eastern Europe had a different education system before the Second World War, with education usually confined to children of the rich. Most of the population could not read or write. The far-reaching political changes after the war meant sweeping transformations in education.

Education began to develop

▲ Nursery schools are very common in all the countries of Eastern Europe. They are cheap and widely available in the towns. This nursery is located in Prague, the capital of Czechoslovakia, where most toddlers attend nursery.

along similar lines to the Soviet system. The aim was to meet the needs of the economy by training young people in certain skills, and to provide equal opportunity for all girls and boys. So there are today no private schools, no single-sex schools and no streaming anywhere in Eastern Europe.

Education is free and open to all children, whatever their background, including higher education. Children therefore generally attend school from six to 17, and many in the towns attend day nursery as well, especially as, in many families, both parents work.

Education is not over when the bell goes. All pupils are normally members of a children's organization from the age of seven, and attend their clubs after school. From the age of ten they are Pioneers, with the right to wear the red neck scarf, and at 15 many join the Young Communist League.

Some special boarding schools exist for handicapped children and for those gifted in art, music, ballet, science and sport. Like all schools, they are completely free.

Higher education

Each country has its older, more traditional universities. Charles University in Prague, for instance, was founded in 1348 and is therefore one of the oldest

universities in Europe.

Since 1945, however, there has been a rapid growth in the number of technical institutes where subjects are more closely related to the needs of industry and farming. It has to be remembered that with the rapid economic changes school and college have to meet the country's needs in technical and scientific personnel.

A major change in higher education has been the huge increase in the number of sons and daughters of farmers and workers who reach university. This is one of the major results of providing equal opportunity for all young people in the free education system.

Practical work for the good of the community is a common feature of student life. Not only do most students spend at least a year of their normally five-year course on practice, but they are also expected to spend part of their summer vacation in helping dig potatoes, bringing in the harvest or in some other socially-useful work.

At the end of a student's course she or he is guaranteed a job, according to the learned skills and qualifications. But students are also expected to work in the job and place to which they are assigned for a minimum of two years, as repayment to society for their education.

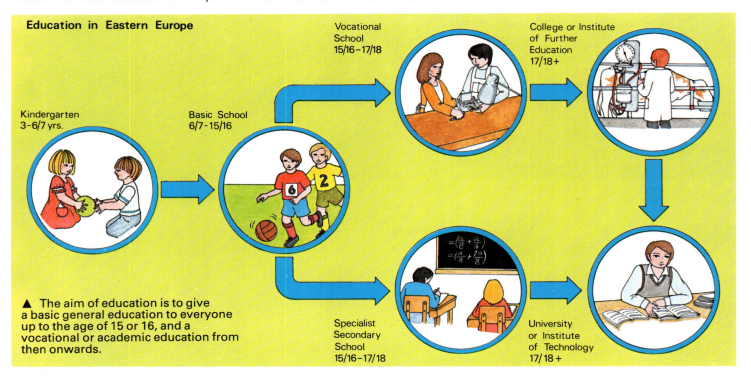

Education in Eastern Europe

Kindergarten 3-6/7 yrs.

Basic School 6/7-15/16

Vocational School 15/16-17/18

College or Institute of Further Education 17/18+

Specialist Secondary School 15/16-17/18

University or Institute of Technology 17/18+

▲ The aim of education is to give a basic general education to everyone up to the age of 15 or 16, and a vocational or academic education from then onwards.

◄ The physics room of a new vocational school at Pelhrimov in southern Czechoslovakia. After leaving school, the apprentices spend part of their time working in a factory and the rest at a trade school like this, where they combine technical with general subjects.

▲ Medical students at Charles University in Prague. One marked feature of the education system is the large proportion of women students in higher education, often studying medicine or engineering.

▼ These are children at school in Bucharest, Romania. Children often wear their Pioneer uniform in school, since many of the Pioneer activities take place at school. The Pioneer motto is the same as the Scouts: Be prepared.

Leisure and sport

More leisure time

Most East Europeans have three or four weeks paid holidays a year and many spend at least some of that time at a holiday resort: some in camps, some in their own wooden cabins, some in hotels or rest homes. It is hard for people to travel to the West because their governments do not encourage such travel. But there are plenty of summer and winter holiday resorts for people to choose from within the region.

If people want a seaside holiday they can go to the Baltic Sea in the north, or the Black Sea or Adriatic in the south. They can also go to the Yugoslav or Bulgarian coast, but since this region has become popular with Western tourists, prices tend to be higher.

If they want breath-taking scenery and a less crowded holiday, there are a large number of mountain areas, such as the Tatras in Czechoslovakia and Poland, which are popular for hiking in summer, and for skiing in winter. There are large skiing centres in the Transylvanian Alps and the Carpathians in Romania, Bulgaria and Yugoslavia.

One of the favourite resorts in central Europe is Lake Balaton in north-west Hungary. It is the largest lake in central Europe and is 112 kilometres from Budapest.

Excellence in sport

Sport is much encouraged by the East European governments. They feel that people will work better if they are healthier, and that they will benefit from the enjoyment of pursuing their favourite sport. Also, success in international sport, especially the Olympic Games, is seen as helping the countries gain respect in the world.

The nations of Eastern Europe and the Soviet Union have dominated recent Olympics, with the GDR winning most medals at the 1980 and 1984 Winter Olympics, and taking more medals than the USA at the 1976 Summer Olympics. At that Olympics, East European nations took six of the top ten places.

The reason for such success lies mainly in sport being free and open to all, and in children with talent being able to develop their gifts at sports schools. The GDR, for example, has some 20 residential sports schools for young people gifted at Olympic sports like gymnastics, ice skating and athletics.

▲ May Day is a popular holiday throughout Eastern Europe, being a celebration of solidarity with workers the world over.

▼ Chess is popular with people of all ages and players may be found almost everywhere you go: from parks to trains, mountain tops to cafes.

▲ Bulgaria is famous for its weightlifters and wrestlers. Several have become world champions.

▲ Ice hockey is a favourite sport in Czechoslovakia and all countries of Eastern Europe that have five or six months of ice and snow each year. This is a match between old rivals: Czechoslovakia v. the Soviet Union.

◄ A hunting party in Poland. Large areas of Eastern Europe are covered in wild forests, with wolves and bears in the more remote areas.

41

Reference

Eastern Europe consists of a group of eight nations sharing common interests that arise from their similar socialist systems of government. Yugoslavia and Albania are more politically independent, but are still regarded as being part of the socialist community because of their government and socialist philosophy.

There are ethnic ties between the eight countries, since most of the people are Slavs – like 70 per cent of the Soviet people to the east. These political and ethnic ties help to overcome the differences in climate and geography between the countries.

The population of Eastern Europe is just less than half that of the Soviet Union, or the USA or Western Europe, but it has a much smaller area.

Similarly, the capital cities of Eastern Europe are generally smaller in population than those of the Soviet Union, USA or Western Europe. Budapest and Bucharest are the only cities with a population

of more than two million. Most cities have just over a million people. Tirana, the capital of Albania is the smallest capital, with 200,000 inhabitants – which would make it quite a small town by Western standards. The biggest capital city, Budapest, has only just over two million people – much smaller than most Western capitals.

A journey from the Baltic Sea in the north down through the mountains of central Europe to the sunny Adriatic and Black Sea in the south provides a more delightful variety of scenery, people and climate than any other part of the European continent.

Eastern Europe: population and land area – a comparison 1985

Eastern Europe
Pop. 136.1m
Area 1,276,000 sq km

Western Europe
Pop. 353.8m
Area 2,127,000 sq km

USSR
Pop. 280.0m
Area 22,402,000 sq km

USA
Pop. 232.1m
Area 9,363,000 sq km
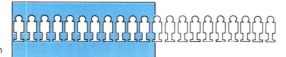

Index